Mer[...] [...]

Linda, Sam,

Hadley & Bevik

2008

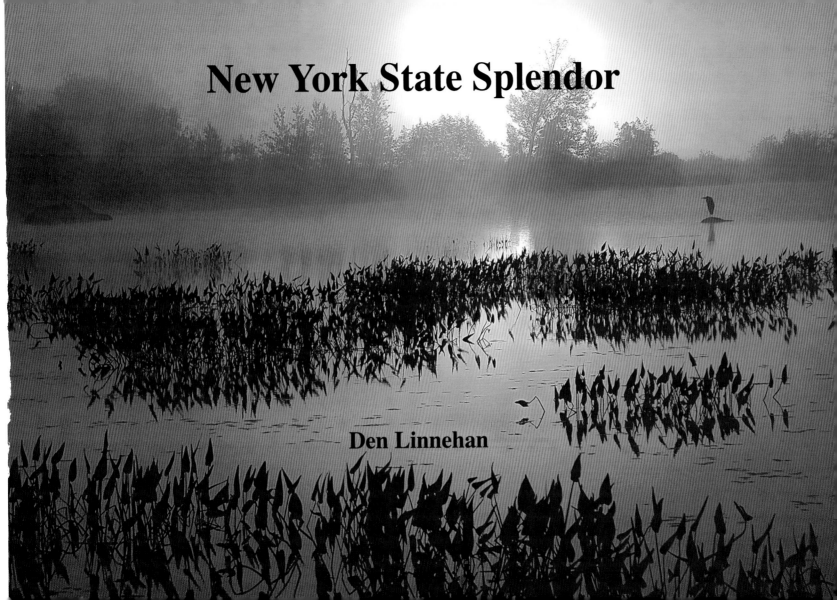

New York State Splendor

Den Linnehan

Published by Linnehan Press 2008
Copyright © 2008 by Den Linnehan
Printed by Monroe Litho

Concept, book design, and all photographs by Den Linnehan with the exception of page 2 photo taken by Barb Ellis.

ISBN 978-0-9740280-3-3

Linnehan, Den   New York State Splendor

Prior photography books include:
Adirondack Splendor
The Finger Lakes: nature's beauty

To order books
Linnehan Press 6833 West Gulick Road Naples, NY 14512
Denlinn@sprynet.com or 585-374-2709

A special thanks to the many organizations, individuals, and businesses that allowed me to photograph their treasures. I wish to thank Rob and Carol Maher for their many hours reviewing the text and photos; there suggestions were most helpful.

Front Cover:	Breakneck Ridge, Hudson Valley
Back Cover:	Bald Mountain, Old Forge, Adirondacks
	Kaaterskill Waterfall, Catskills
	Dead's Man Cove, Southold, Long Island
	Keuka Lake, Finger Lakes
Inside flaps:	Niagara Falls, Southwest Gateway
	Barnes Corner, Thousand Islands
	Central Park, New York City
Page 1:	Piercefield Flow
Page 3:	Big Moose Lake and Lake Placid

This book is dedicated to my aunt and my mother.

Eleanor   Dorothy

Come visit New York State's breathtaking scenery with its varying moods. Here are more than 130 inspiring images of New York State. I'll show you familiar places under unique lighting conditions. I'll show unfamiliar places where beauty abounds. Many landscapes were scouted six or seven times before I obtained the emotion of the scene. Waiting countless hours for the correct cloud formation or angle of the sun's rays is essential. Getting that perfect light is my passion.

I have spent the last 5 years traveling the state. We will visit magnificent thundering waterfalls and whirlpools, beautiful glacier lakes, mighty rivers, and deep gorges in the Southwest Gateway region. In the Finger Lakes we will view unique glens and state parks, spectacular sunrises and sunsets over the glacier carved land. In the Central and Catskill area our trip takes us to sandstone cliffs, beautiful churches, and covered bridges. The Hudson Valley scenes contain some of the most historic sites in the United States as well as formal gardens, stunning stained glass windows, fall hikes, and the mighty Hudson River. In New York City we will visit famous landmarks, landscaped gardens, large parks, famous zoos, and botanical gardens. On Long Island we will discover stunning beaches, magnificent historic estates, old grist mills, lighthouses, wildlife refuges, and a variety of farms and vineyards. Within the 1000 Islands are views of old castles, islands, state parks, and less traveled country roads. In the Adirondacks we will hike mountains for panoramic views at sunrise, canoe lakes and streams, and view stunning waterfalls.

Enjoy this mosaic of moods and majesty that is New York State.

Mist rises from Niagara Falls to shroud the Maid of the Mist boat as it approaches Horseshoe Falls.

This wooden structure allows a close up view of the American Falls from Cave of the Winds. Expect to get wet.

6   Down stream from Niagara Falls is the whirlpool.

Murder Creek in Akron Falls County Park overflowed its banks after a heavy rain.

The Genesee River meanders through Letchworth State Park carving the canyon and creating these dramatic cliffs.

In March a single visitor gazes at the 107 foot Middle Falls.

In summer the Genesee River flows gently over a stone dam near the town of Belmont.

In the village of Williamsville is the 27 foot Glen Falls.

On Red House Lake in Allegany State Park one can swim, canoe, boat, or just enjoy the scenery.

Near Allegany State Park is Jakes Rocks and Little Rock City. It is a labyrinth of large rocks and caves.

An early fall morning at Canandaigua Lake.

Honeoye Lake in late summer shrouded in fog.

The Naples countryside consists of small mountains with fields crisscrossing the landscape.

Billowing clouds suggest an approaching storm over the Bristol Hills.

Buttermilk Creek winds through Buttermilk State Park carving out the glen.

Stony Brook State Park consists of 600 acres of hilly woodlands, gorges, and three major waterfalls.

Harriet Hollister Spencer State Recreation Area overlooks Honeoye Lake in late summer.

Keuka Lake near the town of Hammondsport.

Mountains shrouded in fog near Cohocton.

Many horse farms exist in the Finger Lakes region.

Canadice Lake on a tranquil summer evening.

Apples, too high for the deer to reach, are frozen in an ice and snow wonderland.

Ice fishing on Honeoye Lake.

A spectacular sunset near the town of Naples.

Robert H. Treman State Park with the 115 foot Lucifer Falls.

Water has carved the lower portion of the mile and a half Gorge Trail in Watkins Glen State Park into intricate patterns and shapes.

Taughannock Falls State Park features a 215 foot waterfall.

Buttermilk State Park has numerous small waterfalls within the glen.

Miles of hiking trails dot the shoreline of Otsego Lake in Glimmerglass State Park.

Located near Cooperstown in Glimmerglass State Park is the Hyde Hall Covered Bridge, wrapped in fall foliage.

After a 15 minute hike to the canyon floor this beautiful series of waterfalls is heard and seen in Mine Kill State Park.

The Livingston Manor Covered Bridge is the oldest of four town lattice-truss covered bridges in Sullivan County. 35

After a heavy rain the Chittenango Creek cascades over rock ledges in Chittenango Falls State Park.

Lower Falls in Fillmore Glen State Park.

Located in the Shawangunk Mountains, Minnewaska State Park has miles of hiking trails and boating activities.

Kaaterskill Waterfall is the tallest two stage waterfall in New York State at 260 total feet.

Climbing Sky Top path for less than one mile leads to spectacular views of Eagle Cliff in the distance.

Looking north over Mohonk Lake the Catskill Mountains are visible in the distance.

The Shawangunk Mountains with views of the Albert K. Smiley Memorial Tower.

The Burds Farm stand sells a variety of items throughout each season.

Built in 1854, the Old Blenheim Covered Bridge is 232 feet long, 26 feet wide, and crosses the Schoharie Creek.

Built in 1872, Stone Arch Bridge near Kenoza Lake, is the only bridge of its kind in the United States.

A short steep difficult climb up Breakneck Ridge provides spectacular views along the Hudson River.

One of the many overlooks from Breakneck Ridge with the Hudson River far below.

Stony Point State Park offers numerous views of the Hudson River.

A short hike around Sugarloaf Mountain provides wilderness views of the Hudson Valley.

At Fahnestock Memorial State Park a small pond reflects the sunset.

A moderate hike up Anthony's Nose trail leads to views of the valley below.

Marc Chagall created nine magnificent stained glass windows in the Union Church of Pocantico Hills, three of which are seen here: Elijah, Ezekiel, and Cherubim.

The reconstructed 17th century manor house and grist mill at Phillipsburg Manor.

Next to the Vanderbilt Mansion at Hyde Park are acres of formal gardens.

Spring and fall visits bring different views of Madam Brett Park. Golden leaves signal the fall season.

Camoon Klinger and friend test their skills below the main falls in Madam Brett Park.

Central Park contains over 800 acres of landscaped and wooded grounds.

Many formal areas exist within the winding walkways of Central Park.

From Vista Rock, Belvedere Castle overlooks the Great Lawn area of Central Park and the New York City skyline.

At the Bethesda Fountain and Terrace water lilies bloom in late summer.

The building bears the inscription "ENID A. HAUPT CONSERVATORY" and "MDCCCXCIX" with "A World of Plants" above the entrance doors.

The 250 acre New York Botanical Gardens includes the Victorian style Enid Haupt Conservatory.

Eleven greenhouses and numerous large pools surround the conservatory.

Twenty eight outdoor gardens feature native plants, roses, perennials, and a 50 acre forest.

The Bronx Zoo contains 265 acres and houses over 4,000 animals in large open areas.

Giraffes.

A tiger drinks his fill at a small watering hole at the Bronx Zoo.

A polar bear shakes water off his thick fur after a casual swim.

Grand Central Station.

Rockefeller Plaza at Christmas time.

Fire Island Lighthouse is located in Robert Moses State Park on Long Island.

Climb 132 lighthouse steps for views of the Atlantic Ocean, Fire Island Inlet, and Great South Bay.

On a clear summer day the entire 32 mile island is visible by walking around the top of Fire Island Lighthouse.

Jones Beach stretches for five miles. It is quiet and calm after Labor Day.

The Old Westbury House, the former home of John S. Phipps, as viewed from the manicured South Terrace.

Within the 160 acres of Old Westbury are tree lined walkways, lakes, and the walled garden seen here.

The Southold Horton Point Lighthouse overlooks Southold Bay and a portion of Long Island Sound.

Glacial boulders lie just beneath the surface and on the shore of Dead Man's Cove.

Views of Orient Beach West Harbor, near Oyster Bay.

In Centerport, the historic Vanderbilt Museum and house, overlook Northport Bay.

Intricate stone patterns form a walkway to the main entrance at Eagle's Nest.

Pindar Vineyards in Peconic, with over 500 acres, produce more than 60,000 cases of fine varietal wines.

Hayground Farmers Market displays the fruits and vegetables of the fall season.

Elizabeth A. Morton National Wildlife Refuge protects migratory birds and mammals.

A flat walk of less than one third of a mile leads to Little Peconic Bay.

Noyack Creek is seen from the beach and dunes of Elizabeth A. Morton National Wildlife Refuge.

The "walking dunes" at Hither Hills State Park. Strong winds move the dunes over three feet each year.

The Hook Windmill was built by Nathaniel Dominy V. in 1806 on the Memorial Green in East Hampton.

A Sag Harbor sunrise viewed from the 1,000 foot Long Wharf area.

Sag Harbor Whaling and Historical Museum is a fine example of Greek Revival with ornate Corinthian columns.

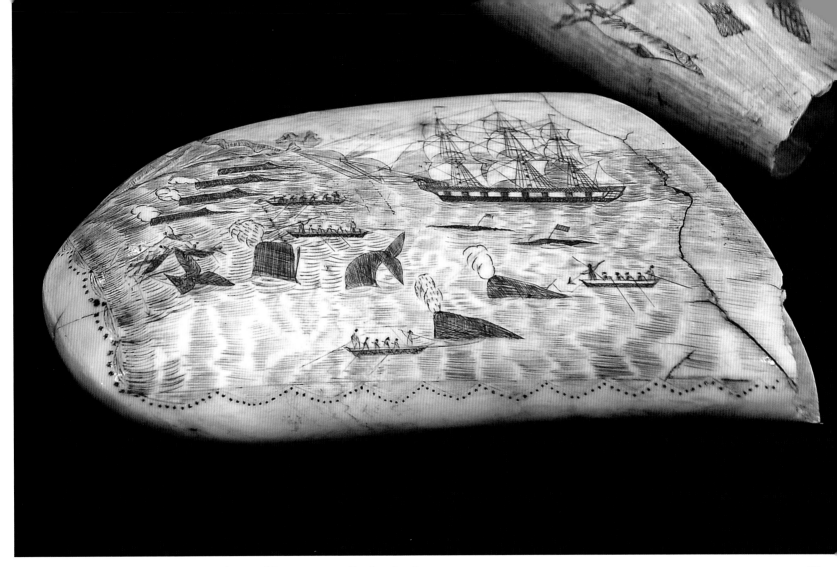

Scrimshaw and whaling artifacts are on display in the museum.

Fishing is popular near the Montauk Point Lighthouse.

Camp Hero State Park and beach area at sunrise.

Chris Anderson plays the bagpipes for a wedding within the Montauk Point Lighthouse grounds.

Montauk Point Lighthouse near dawn. Constructed in 1796, it was the first New York State lighthouse.

Over 300 construction workers built Boldt Castle - a six story replica of a Rhineland castle.

Boldt Castle's interior staircase and second floor balcony. About eighty percent of the castle is restored now.

The Thousand Islands consists of over 1800 islands. Size varies greatly from a few square feet to some 20 miles long.

Near the town of Barnes Corners on the Tug Hill Plateau many dirt roads become snowmobile trails in winter.

As fall fades, fallen leaves freeze into icy intricate patterns.

Tug Hill Plateau in early October experiences its first frost.

The Erwin Park Boonville Covered Bridge allows one to hike the Black River Feeder Canal Towpath trail.

Pixley State Park contains a 50 foot waterfall and is a great place to hike steeply wooded hills, picnic, or camp.

Bald Mountain near Old Forge at sunrise.

Rocky Mountain near Inlet. At sunrise the fog covered the entire mountain.

Sunset at Arrowhead Park in the town of Inlet.

Shaw Pond near the town of Long Lake.

On a cold gloomy day, for one brief moment, the sun lit up Big Moose Lake.

Tupper Lake mist rise.

A unique mist rise in the town of Lake Placid near the golf course.

On the ADK LOJ road sunset illuminates plants awaiting harvest. Cascade Mountain is in the background.

Heart Lake near the peak of the fall season.

At sunrise clouds obscured the high peaks in waves.

The Lake George area near the start of the Black Mountain trail.

Schroon Lake at sunrise.

Lichens cover the rocks near Hammond Pond.

Fall foliage reflects in Hammond Pond.

The sun rising over Jay Covered Bridge. The bridge restoration was completed in 2007.

Paul Smiths Visitor Information Center has numerous relatively flat trails to hike.

Near County Route 45 in the Adirondacks fall turns the lily pads a golden hue.

Water levels were very low at Great Sacandaga Lake creating this interesting pattern in the sand.

Indian Head with views of Colvin and Sawteeth Mountain with Lower and Upper Ausable Lakes visible below.

A short but steep hike of less than one quarter mile leads to Stag Brook Waterfall in the Whiteface ski area.

To travel from Heart Lake to Avalanche Lake one must negotiate huge boulders in Avalanche Pass.

Cascade Mountain Waterfall wedged between Lower and Upper Cascade Ponds flows after a heavy rain.

Rainbow Waterfall near the town of Saint Huberts within the Adirondack Mountain Preserve.